PORTVILLE FREE LIBRARY
Portville, New York 14770

D0850096

The Bushmen of the Kalahari

The Bushmen are hunter-gatherers who have lived in Africa for at least 20,000 years. Over the centuries their unique lifestyle has enabled them to adapt to changing environments and, until the arrival of white settlers three hundred years ago, they were found all over southern Africa. The Europeans built farms on their lands and forced the Bushmen away from their traditional hunting grounds. They now live mainly in the Kalahari Desert region, still retaining their hunter-gatherer way of life and many traditions of their prehistoric ancestors. But their future is far from secure. This book looks at the history and present-day circumstances of the Bushmen, including the effects of war on Namibia's northern border, which directly affects them. Dr. Steyn is a former lecturer in anthropology at Stellenbosch University. He is an authority on the Bushmen and has worked among them in Botswana and Namibia.

Original
Peoples

THE BUSHMEN
OF THE KALAHARI

H.P. Steyn

DISCARDED FROM THE
PORTVILLE FREE LIBRARY

Rourke Publications, Inc.
Vero Beach, FL 32964

Original Peoples

Eskimos — The Inuit of the Arctic
Maoris of New Zealand
Aborigines of Australia
Plains Indians of North America
South Pacific Islanders
Indians of the Andes
Indians of the Amazon
Bushmen of the Kalahari
Pygmies of Central Africa
Bedouin — The Nomads of the Desert
The Zulus of Southern Africa

Frontispiece *A Bushman returning from the hunt.*

Library of Congress Cataloging-in-Publication Data

Steyn, H.P. (Hendrik Pieter)
  The bushmen of the Kalahari / H.P. Steyn.
    p.   cm.— (Original peoples)
  Reprint. Originally published: Hove, East Sussex,
England : Wayland, 1985.
    Bibliography: p.
    Includes index
    Summary: Introduces the history, culture, and daily
life of the hunter-gatherers who have lived in Africa for
20,000 years.
    ISBN 0–86625–267–3
    1. San (African people) — Juvenile literature. [1. San
(African people) 2. Kalahari Desert.]   I. Title.
II. Series.
[DT764.B8S752 1989]
968.1′.1004961–dc19   88–15072
                                          CIP
                                          AC

Printed in Italy by Tipolitografia G. Canale & C. S.p.A. - Turin
Text © 1989 Rourke Publications, Inc.

All rights reserved. No part of this book may be
reproduced or utilized in any form or by any
means, electronic or mechanical, including
photocopying and recording, or by any information
storage and retrieval system without permission
in writing from the publisher.

Contents

Introduction

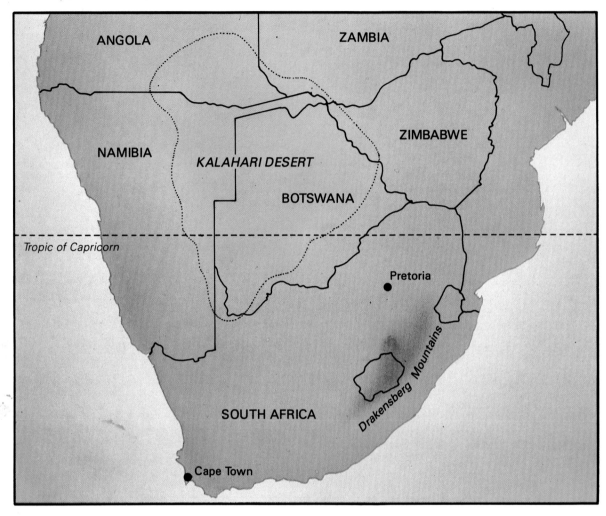

Southern Africa, showing the area of the Kalahari Desert where the Bushmen still live.

The Bushmen — also known as *San* by their *Khoi* neighbors — are among the world's best-known hunter-gatherers. They have been living in large areas of southern Africa for thousands of years, which shows how remarkably well they have been able to adapt to the various environments in which they have lived. These have included the wet coastal regions, the dry Karoo shrubland, the grassy plains of the Highveld, the bare Namib desert strip and the Kalahari Sandveld (Desert). They are now found only in the Kalahari.

The Bushmen once shared the western parts of southern Africa with the *Khoi* who, like them, had yellow-brown skins and spoke in

1655, today they live more than 600 miles (1,000 kilometers) away in the Kalahari, their last stronghold. They number an estimated 50,000 or more, but their traditional lifestyle is changing very rapidly.

Below *A woman from the northern Kalahari. She shows how the Bushmen make elaborate use of ornaments.*

Above *This Bushman from the central Kalahari is typically well-built, with yellow-brown skin and slant eyes.*

click languages. However, the life-styles of these two groups of people were very different. The *Khoi*, unlike the Bushmen, kept large herds of cattle and sheep.

The name "Bushmen" was given to them by early Dutch settlers at the Cape, either because they lived in the bush or because they used an aromatic powder made from certain bushes.

Although settlers found the Bushmen living near Cape Town in

Chapter 1 **The Bushmen in history**

Who were they and how did they live?

The Bushmen are hunter-gatherers, descended from the prehistoric population that has lived in southern Africa for several hundred thousand years. It is difficult for us to link living Bushmen with their prehistoric ancestors from the archaeological evidence we have, but they have probably been living in southern Africa for at least 20,000 years.

The way of life of today's Bushmen seems to resemble that of prehistoric hunter-gatherers in many ways. The rock shelters that are found all over southern Africa show that hunter-gatherers have used much the same artifacts for the last 10,000 years. Stone tools and many other objects made from bone, wood, ostrich eggshell, marine shells and sinew have been found.

The Kalahari Bushmen are hunter-gatherers, living in much the same way as their prehistoric ancestors.

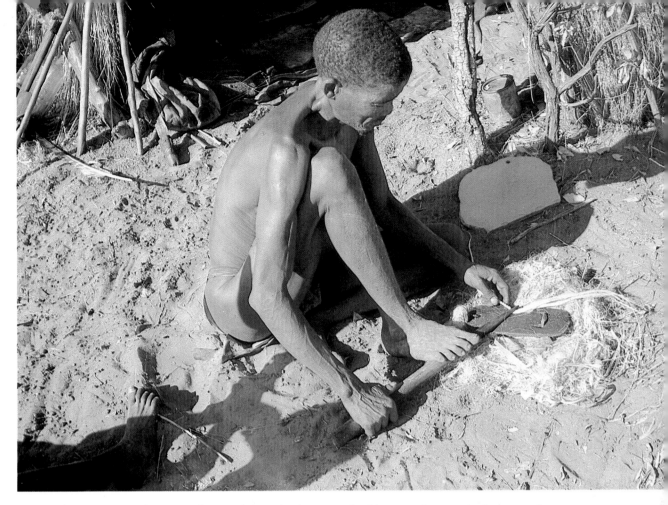

A Bushman strips the outer layers from the leaves of a fibrous plant in order to make rope for animal snares.

Food remains show that they ate various plants and animals, and probably moved about in small groups, searching for food. They lived by hunting, snaring, gathering and fishing.

The Portuguese navigator, Bartholomew Diaz, and his crew were the first Europeans to set foot on South African soil, when they landed in the southern Cape in 1488. The local inhabitants, who were probably *Khoi* people, immediately fled inland.

Another Portuguese, Vasco da Gama, landed on the Cape's west coast in 1497. He met people who had no cattle and who gathered plant foods and honey, hunted antelope and ate seal and whale meat. These may have been the first Bushmen seen by Europeans.

During the next 150 years, many seamen visited the Cape shore. A flourishing trade grew between them and the cattle-owning *Khoi* people. Since trading was carried out mostly on the beaches, the visiting seamen rarely penetrated the interior of the country.

Rock art

There are thousands of prehistoric rock art sites in southern Africa, and some paintings date back more than 25,000 years. Many of the paintings and engravings are beautiful works of art depicting the lifestyle of the people who made them. The animals which were part of their environment and which they hunted are portrayed, as are their hunting techniques, food-gathering, dances, and some of their religious rituals. A few of the paintings that were made in recent history, depict settlers, ships, horsemen, women in long dresses, and ox wagons.

This beautiful painting can be found in a rock shelter in Namibia. It depicts hunters with their bows and arrows fleeing from a charging rhinoceros.

Although it is not certain who the artists were in all cases, most paintings and engravings are believed to be the work of Bushmen because many of the themes portrayed were important to prehistoric hunter-gatherers. Most of the paintings are red or reddish brown, but there are also yellow, white and black paintings. The artists mixed their paints from rocks, sand and plants.

Why did the hunter-gatherers paint? There may have been several reasons. One of the most frequently portrayed subjects was the eland, an animal that may have had a special symbolic importance for the Bushmen. Other paintings may have been made simply because the artist wanted to record an important event, such as a memorable hunt, a battle scene or a ritual dance, perhaps to celebrate the visit of a neighboring group.

Unfortunately, the painting tradition, like the Bushmen artists, has now died out. The living Kalahari Bushmen do not practice rock art. But they do make small engravings on some of their utensils, such as ostrich-eggshell containers, which are then rubbed with fat and charcoal to make the design clearer.

A painting of two giraffes, one showing the typical color pattern of the skin.

Chapter 2 **The arrival of the Europeans**

Early contacts

The first contact with, and the first description of, people who were unmistakably Bushmen was made by Jan Wintervogel and his men during an expedition in 1655 into the interior north of Cape Town. They described the people that they found there as small, lean, clad in skins, without any huts or cattle. To the Dutchmen, they appeared to be wild savages. The explorers, however, found these hunter-gatherers to be very friendly. The Bushmen exchanged honey and rock rabbits for tobacco. When the Governor at the Cape, Simon van der Stel, traveled north in 1685, he presented a group of Bushmen with a sheep. In return he received animal skins.

The weapons of the Bushmen

The first European settlers came to South Africa in the mid-seventeenth century. This picture shows Cape Town in those early days.

Simon van der Stel, Governor of the Cape in 1685, prepares for his journey into the northern part of the province.

consisted of bows, arrows and spears. Their most important foods were wild plants and the meat of animals that they hunted. Among these were small creatures such as rock rabbits and tortoises. Honey seems to have been a favorite supplementary item on the Bushmen menu.

It is very sad that so little has been recorded about the way of life of the Bushmen met by travelers during those early years. Except for some brief remarks about the number of Bushmen they saw, the early explorers simply commented on how few possessions they had, their small stature, their weapons and some of their foods. Nobody was interested enough to learn more about their way of life.

On the other hand, we do have many descriptions of how the relationship between these people and the Dutch settlers deteriorated during this period.

Many settlers moved inland, away from the Cape, and took over traditional Bushmen hunting and gathering territories.

Conflict

Since the early days of the Dutch settlement at the Cape, the Bushmen had a reputation for thieving. This was because the local *Khoi* herders complained that the Bushmen stole their cattle. Despite the Bushmen's reputation, quarrels between the hunter-gatherers and the *Khoi* herders seem to have been few, and they probably lived together peacefully most of the time.

As settlers started moving inland, conflict with the Bushmen gradually increased. Not only did they settle in areas that were the Bushmen's traditional hunting and gathering territories, but they also shot and reduced the herds of wild game that the Bushmen hunted for food.

The Bushmen probably considered that the cattle and sheep were easier to hunt than the wild game that was no longer available to them. They would even kill herdsmen who defended the cattle. From the settlers' point of view, the Bushmen had to be punished. This situation led to increasing conflict on both sides.

In the early 1700s, the settlers introduced the commando system, which involved military action by groups of farmers on horseback. The commandos proved to be highly effective against the Bushmen. The normal method used by the commandos was to send out scouts to locate Bushmen caves or settlements. In most cases, the Bushmen would not surrender, so the commandos would surround and attack these settlements. Since the Bushmen had only arrows, and, in the mountains, boulders which they rolled down on their attackers, their weapons proved to be no match for the rifle fire of the commandos. Hundreds of Bushmen were killed, while many others were taken away as prisoners.

A nineteenth-century illustration of some Bushmen.

Chapter 3 **The last South African Bushmen**

The Drakensberg Bushmen

Many settlers left the eastern Cape during the 1830s. After moving inland to present-day Lesotho, they turned toward the coast and moved into what is today the Province of Natal. Here they clashed with the armies of the Zulu king, Dingane.

The settlers won a decisive battle against the Zulus in December 1838, and large areas of Natal became available for settlement. The farmers who settled close to the Drakensberg mountain range found history repeating itself when their cattle were again raided by Bushmen.

The Drakensberg mountains form a nearly impenetrable fortress that reaches a height of more than 9,842 feet (3,000 meters) and stretches a distance of some 124 miles (200 kilometers). It was impossible to find the Bushmen, who fled to higher ground and vanished into the labyrinth of peaks and valleys, which only they knew intimately.

By the end of the nineteenth century, the Drakensberg Bushmen had mostly vanished, mainly because of population pressure from Sotho tribesmen who expanded their territories into the higher ground of the Drakensberg. Eventually they reached the remotest areas, which were the last refuge of the Bushmen.

The Bushmen were unable to maintain their ancient hunter-

The settlers moved into Natal where some of them farmed lands near the impenetrable Drakensberg mountains.

gatherer lifestyle because so much wild game had been taken and their traditional territories were occupied either by Sotho or white settlers. Because they were so few and scattered, the Drakensberg Bushmen could not support themselves as a separate population and they were eventually absorbed by the Sotho settlers.

The Drakensberg today is a monument to them. There, there are thousands of rock shelters containing some of the most beautiful rock art ever created by prehistoric and historic hunter-gatherers.

Although the Bushmen have vanished from the Drakensberg, they have left behind monuments in the form of beautiful rock paintings.

The Southern Transvaal Bushmen

During the 1950s a few individual Bushmen still lived in the south-eastern Transvaal Province of South Africa. Their ancestors had probably been living in this area before the arrival of the neighboring Swazi tribespeople or the white settlers. Here, as elsewhere, the Bushmen were simply pushed off the land.

By the 1850s, white settlers had moved into the area. As they settled on what they must have regarded as unoccupied land, the ancient hunting and gathering territories of the Bushmen soon shrank. It therefore did not take long before the Bushmen, who had been roaming freely over the land, hunting and trapping the springbok, blesbok and other plains game and collecting various food plants, began to settle on the farms, working as farm laborers.

Some of the descendants of these Bushmen survive, but they have all lost their traditional culture and language. The Transvaal Bushmen can today be considered to have died out completely as a distinct population group.

Lost between two worlds — a farm Bushman who leads a settled life. In the background is a typical Bushman hut.

Bushmen of the north-western Cape

One of the last of the Cape Bushmen.

In 1937, the South African public suddenly became aware of the nearly forgotten Bushmen when a group from the southern Kalahari was exhibited in Johannesburg. These were some of the last Cape Bushmen, who at that time probably numbered less than two hundred and lived in a remote corner of the northwestern Cape Province.

Because the Bushmen lived in an isolated, sparsely inhabited corner of the country, very little notice had been paid to them. In the dune country of the southern Kalahari they could still roam freely, hunting game and obtaining the water they needed by eating moisture-bearing plants. But, like Bushmen elsewhere in South Africa, they were doomed to extinction because their hunting territories were in an area where a huge game reserve was proclaimed in 1931.

Without any land rights, the Bushmen had no future. Today, they and their children work as farm hands, servants, trackers and shepherds.

Chapter 4 **The Kalahari Bushmen**

Their distribution and numbers

The Kalahari Bushmen are in no danger of dying out. Today they are found within the borders of several countries, and number more than 50,000 people. Between 20,000 and 40,000 of them live in Botswana, while Namibia has a Bushman population of between 10,000 and 20,000. Several thousand Bushmen used to live in Angola, but because a prolonged bush war has been raging in their traditional living areas for many years, their present situation is not known.

The fact that the Kalahari Bushmen have survived to the present day is due largely to their own abilities and to the fact that they were isolated within the dry Kalahari areas, which were unattractive to both black and white settlers.

This isolation has now been broken, and despite their numbers, the ultimate cultural survival of the Bushmen is again in doubt. We know from what has happened to other Bushmen that they could not

Two hunters setting a snare to catch a steenbok.

PORTVILLE FREE LIBRARY

Portville, New York 14770

A Bushman and his wife in a Kalahari settlement. Their possessions include pestle and mortar and ostrich-eggshell container. Skins of hunted animals are spread out to dry.

survive as a cultural group without their traditional territories.

All of the Bushmen may soon find themselves employed by black or white farmers who own the land that has belonged to the Bushmen for thousands of years. In fact, hundreds of Bushmen are today unemployed squatters on farms developed in their old hunting territories.

All Bushmen are traditional hunter-gatherers, but there are many small cultural differences among the various groups. Their languages all have the characteristic click sounds, but they may differ so much in other ways that Bushmen belonging to different language groups may not be able to understand each other.

21

A Bushman camp in the northern Kalahari, consisting of several grass-covered shelters.

The Kalahari environment

The Kalahari Desert covers an immense area. Due to an increase in rainfall from south to north, the northern Kalahari has a dense, bushveld type of vegetation, while the southern Kalahari is drier, with sparse, savanna-type vegetation. In the south, red sand dunes occur, while the central and northern Kalahari is mostly flat with light-colored sand.

To the Bushmen, who have adapted to all parts of the Kalahari, life is easier in the northern region, where rainfall is higher, water more accessible and food plants more plentiful than it is in the southern Kalahari. But all Kalahari Bushmen have to cope with water and food shortages for at least part of the year. The time before the summer rains is the annual period of hardship, during which Bushmen have to rely on their knowledge of the environment more than at any other time.

They cope with these circumstances in several ways — by splitting into smaller camps, by moving camp more often in order to live off larger areas, by spending more time hunting small, non-migrating game and by eating less desirable foods, such as baked animal skins, which they store for the leaner times. This way, Bushmen have survived successfully in the Kalahari Desert for thousands of years.

Although, to the outsider, the desert seems a hostile and even dangerous area, it supports many water-bearing and food plants and wild animals. Because animals often migrate and are difficult to hunt, food plants form the main part of the diet of most Kalahari Bushmen. Plants may also be the main, and sometimes the only, source of moisture for up to nine months of the year.

This Bushman and other members of his camp will eat every scrap of meat from the animal he has killed.

A group of Bushmen who share the same camp.

Social grouping

Human beings are social animals, and the Bushmen are no exception. They prefer to live together in groups which often consist of related families. These family groups are

usually quite small, but may vary in size from twelve members or less to around fifty. The size of the groups alters continuously, often because of the changes in availability of food and water in a particular territory.

Moving from one group to

another is an important technique of survival for the Bushmen. It maintains a balance between the number of people and the often limited supply of food within a particular territory.

Due to the network of family ties that often links various local groups, Bushmen who leave one group can very easily join another. Sometimes members of a group may quarrel among themselves, which may cause them to leave one group and stay temporarily with another. Some Bushmen may also spend a considerable part of the year visiting relatives and friends with whom they may stay for several months before deciding to move on again.

The size of their groups varies a great deal, and the group members change throughout the year. This is why the Bushmen place great emphasis on the value of being able to adapt to one another and the ability to live in harmony together. Their custom of sharing the meat of a large animal with other members of the camp demonstrates this basic value.

The Bushmen need to get along well together, and they adjust easily to living in different groups.

A Central Kalahari Bushman playing his musical bow.

Settlements

Bushmen move their camps depending on their food, water and social needs, so they do not waste much time and energy in building huts. These are small domes with a framework of branches covered with a layer of grass. From a distance they look like a cluster of small haystacks. These flimsy structures protect the Bushmen from cold and also serve as storerooms for their clothing and utensils. In winter they make a small fire near the hut entrance, around which they huddle during cold nights. If they are on the move, they may not bother to build huts but camp under trees or make small windbreaks of grass around their sleeping places.

Huts usually belong to families, although elderly couples or teenage children may live in separate huts. The huts belonging to members of an extended family are usually placed next to each other. Although there is no regular pattern in the layout of the settlement, huts are often placed in a circle, leaving a central open space, which the Bushmen use for communal activities, such as ritual dancing.

Except for hunting and gathering, daily activities take place near the cooking fires in front of the huts. Here, the men prepare hunting equipment, tan animal skins and sew them into karosses (clocks). The women make ostrich-eggshell beads, which they use to fashion jewelery and decorate garments. They also prepare food for their families on the cooking fire or using wooden pestles and mortars. Families gather here with other relatives and friends to share food, smoke and talk. It is here, too, that babies are breast fed, passed around and cuddled.

A Bushman couple in the entrance to their hut, surrounded by their few possessions.

Bushmen boys learn the skills of hunting at an early age. These two have just caught a springbok in a metal trap.

Growing up

Bushmen children are usually brought up in a free and easy sort of way. They are not expected to do any hard work. Parents are very lenient and rarely punish their children, although they may scold them occasionally. The children are trained by the example of their parents and elders. They grow up in adult company and are protected by all the members of a Bushmen group from the time they are born.

Mothers often carry their babies with them when they go out to collect food, while older children may stay behind at the settlement under the watchful eye of a grandparent or other adult. At the settlement, the children spend their day playing or listening to stories told to them by the old people.

When they are strong enough, the chidren often accompany their parents on food-collecting or hunting trips. The girls are taught to gather edible plants, while the boys improve their knowledge of hunting and animal behavior. At the age of twelve to fifteen, the children will have learned all the knowledge and skills they need, not only to survive in the veld but also to supply food for a family. They will probably need these skills because many of them, especially the girls, will marry and start to bring up a family soon after the age of puberty.

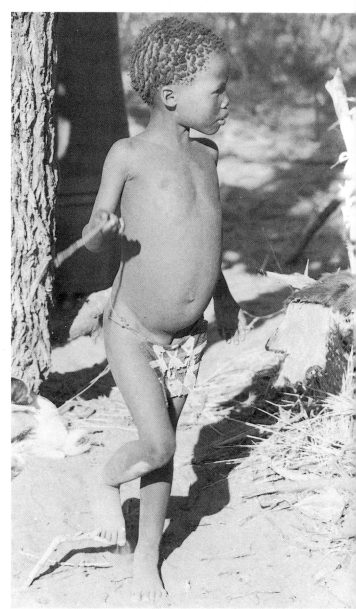

Above *A small girl wearing her traditional apron decorated with beads.*

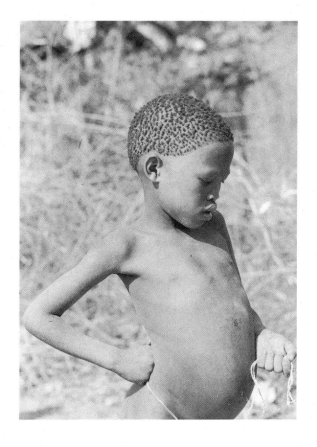

Left *The boys grow up to be fast and skillful hunters.*

This hunter has collected a load of feathers after a successful ostrich hunt.

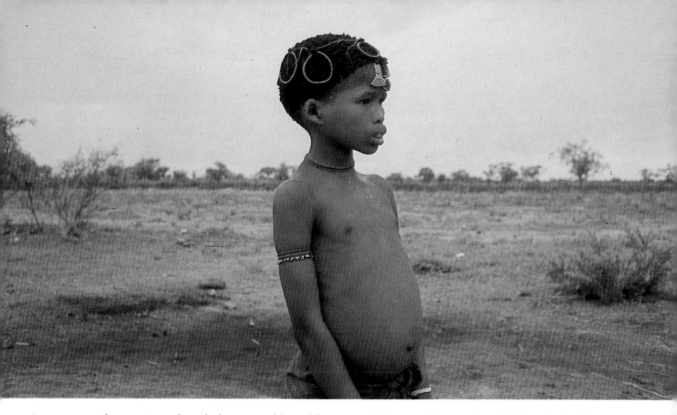

A young girl wearing a bead-decorated headdress, necklace and bracelet. Although she is young, she may well be betrothed to a young hunter.

Marriage

Bushmen boys and girls may be betrothed to each other at a very young age. Marriage partners are often selected by the parents, who look particularly for such qualities as friendliness and adaptability. Harmonious relationships are very important to the Bushmen because they live in small groups and have to see each other every day.

After marriage a man must serve his in-laws with a period of "bride-service." This means that the newly married couple must live in the camp of the bride's parents, and the husband must provide his in-laws with meat. This period of bride-service may last several years, and afterward the couple is free to settle elsewhere if they wish to.

Men are able to marry more than one woman, but this doesn't happen very often, mainly because wives take a dim view of their husband's intentions and will do their best to discourage them from taking another wife.

Although marriage partners may be related, certain close kin may not marry each other. Some Kalahari Bushmen do not allow marriage between cousins.

Many marriages end in divorce. Both partners may remarry, but as they get older, marriage bonds are more likely to become permanent.

These grazing wildebeest in the southern Kalahari are fair game for Bushmen hunters.

Hunting

Today's Bushmen are more gatherers than hunters because they live mainly on food plants. However, they like to eat meat because it brings variety to their dull vegetable diet. The men, therefore, are constantly encouraged to hunt by their parents-in-law and their wives.

They rarely kill large animals, so it is usually the small or medium-sized creatures that provide meat. The importance of certain animals to their diet varies in different parts of the Kalahari according to the species of animals found.

In the southern Kalahari, the gemsbok, springbok, duiker and steenbok are important sources of meat. In the northern Kalahari, animals such as the warthog and kudu are particularly important.

Generally, Bushmen will hunt all plains game, including larger antelope like the eland, wildebeest and hartebeest, and an occasional giraffe. They also hunt small animals such as porcupines, springhares and hares. They collect tortoises and some species of snake, and hunt several types of birds including ostrich, korhaan, francolin and guinea-fowl. They also eat frogs and insects.

Large animals are hunted with bows and poisoned arrows. Most Kalahari groups use the larvae of certain beetles as poison for their arrows. The contents of the larvae are squeezed onto the arrowhead and allowed to dry. This forms an effective poison. Bushmen also snare small antelope, and they hook burrowing animals and drag them out of their burrows with saplings tied together with a hook at one end. Sometimes they trap small animals by lighting fires in their burrows. Many hunters also have metal-bladed spears, which they use to kill wounded animals.

A Bushman prepares his arrows, sharpening their tips and spreading them with poison made from insects' larvae.

Gathering

Among the Bushmen, the women are the actual "breadwinners" because they bring home to the settlement most of the daily food in the form of edible plants.

Although the Kalahari is a dry area, it nevertheless contains a great number and variety of food plants, increasing in number from north to south of the region. In the northern Kalahari the Bushmen eat nearly a hundred different types of plants.

One of the most important is the mongongo nut, which is a principal food of the Bushmen. These nuts provide more than half of the Bushmen's daily diet.

Unlike the Bushmen of the northern Kalahari, where the main food plants are mostly above ground, the Bushmen of the central and southern Kalahari rely a great deal on underground bulbs and tubers for their food and water. In order to find them, the women need to aquire a very detailed knowledge

Although they are sometimes hard to find, underground roots are worth searching for because they provide valuable food and water.

This boy is enjoying a roasted root.

of their desert environment. It takes a lot of hard work and effort to dig out the plant roots, and the women use special digging sticks for the purpose. Each woman carries her daily "crop" of food plants home in her kaross, which usually has enough space left for a few pieces of firewood for the evening's fire.

Gathering firewood is a daily task performed by the women.

A bulb must be prepared so it can be squeezed and moisture taken from it.

Preparing food

The Bushmen prepare food when they need it and as it fits in with their activities. Hunters usually roast the liver and meat of an animal immediately after a successful hunt. The people in the settlement will prepare and cook food in a more leisurely way.

A woman shares out the food plants that she has collected among members of her family. Some kinds of food need to be softened before eating by pounding with a pestle in a wooden mortar, while others are roasted in hot ashes before being shared by the family. Nuts are cracked with stones.

If food is scarce, the women will make daily collecting trips. They return to the settlement in the afternoon and then the sound of the pestle and mortar can be heard until late in the evening.

When food is plentiful, a woman can collect enough food in a single day to feed her family for several days. This gives her an opportunity to spend more time making beads or garments for the children and taking part in gossip and conversation — an activity the talkative Bushmen engage in often.

Meat is either cooked in a pot or metal container, or roasted in the ashes of the fire. Marrowbones and animal heads are also roasted in this way and are eaten with great enjoyment. Not a morsel is wasted.

The meat of a large animal is normally shared among members of the group, who spend pleasant hours around their fires, preparing and cooking the meat. While they cook, they discuss their experiences of the day, sharing them with an always attentive audience.

Below *These melon seeds are ready to be roasted in the fire.*

Above *The tsama melon is an important food and a source of water.*

Skills

Bushmen do not manufacture many items, but their few artifacts are well proven and have ensured the survival of their creators over thousands of years. Since the Bushmen groups frequently move camp, they limit their possessions to what can be carried by the people of the group. This means that they have few possessions. Apart from their huts, which they abandon after a comparatively short time, Bushmen have just the clothes they wear, a few personal belongings that they keep in skin bags, and their hunting, gathering and food-processing equipment.

Bushmen make their clothing from animal skins. Men wear loincloths and women wear aprons. Both sexes may wear skin karosses to keep them warm on cold days. The

Cutting a thong from a piece of animal skin with a knife.

Pegging out a jackal skin, which when it is dry will be softened and made into a cap.

women also use the kaross for carrying their babies and transporting plants to the camp.

Traditionally, all artifacts are made from raw material that is locally available, such as wood, bone, stone and skin. The Bushmen make arrows, bows, mortars, shafts for spears and musical instruments from wood. Arrowheads, pipes for smoking and knives used to be made from bone, but most of these are now made from metal. Stone is used to sharpen arrowheads, knives, the blades of spears and also for polishing the surfaces of ostrich-eggshell beads.

Bushmen manufacture most of their clothing and bags from animal skins. They use sinew for bowstrings, for thread and for the strings of musical instruments. Ostrich eggshells are used for carrying water, and tortoise shells may be used as ladles or water containers.

A trance cure dance that may last all night.

Religion

Bushmen believe in the existence of supernatural beings that influence their lives. Most Kalahari groups believe in a supreme god, creator of the world, and in a lesser being who is usually believed to bring misfortune, sickness, suffering and death. They also believe in life after death, and that people enter the world of the spirits when they die.

The Bushmen believe they can overcome the evil influence of the spirits of the dead and that they can cure sick people by trance cure dancing.

These dances take place in an open space, with the women sitting in a small circle around the fire, and the men dancing in a circle around them. Although the dances may begin in an informal and playful way, the tension and tempo soon build. The men, wearing rattles around their legs, dance to the musical accompaniment of the women, who sing and clap their hands in rhythm.

Eventually, some of the men may work themselves into a state of trance, during which they are believed to be able to cure sick people by touching them and drawing out the disease.

The trance cure dances will often last right through the night. They sometimes leave the Bushmen so exhausted that they are unable to hunt or carry out their usual activities the following day.

The Bushmen believe in a supreme god, creator of the beautiful environment in which they live.

Chapter 5 The future of the Bushmen

Changing culture

For many centuries, the Kalahari Bushmen lived in the protective isolation of the desert where settlers could not survive. However, because of population pressure and the need for more farming lands, the region has recently been settled by people from other areas. Boreholes have opened up large parts of the Kalahari to cattle farmers who have moved into areas previously occupied only by the Bushmen.

This new settlement in the Kalahari is now almost total. There are only two areas, the Central Kalahari Reserve in Botswana, and the so-called Bushmanland in Namibia, where the land rights of Bushmen are positively protected. These are very small parts of the regions over which the Bushmen once used to hunt and gather. Today, thousands are cattle-herders, farm laborers or landless squatters on farmlands that used to form part of their traditional territories.

The future of these Bushmen and their descendants is far from certain.

Farmers have moved into parts of the Kalahari, and the desert is no longer isolated.

Because they have always lived in small, scattered groups that lacked strong leadership, and have been regarded by many as second-class citizens whose rights did not deserve protection, a great many Bushmen have been deprived of their territories. This has resulted in a complete change in the age-old pattern of their lives.

The Bushmen of the northern Kalahari have also been affected by war in their region, and many have fled from Angola to Namibia. Some have enlisted in the army that is fighting a bush war against members of SWAPO (South West Africa Peoples' Organization) in the north of Namibia. These Bushmen soldiers receive good salaries that they sometimes spend unwisely — alcoholism is one of their problems. Perhaps their greatest problem is the uncertainty of the future.

The future

The traditional Bushman way of life has a very bleak future. A large number of Bushmen have already lost much of their traditional culture. Most have also lost their territories, with only a small number remaining on land that is seen as belonging exclusively to Bushmen. Many Bushmen, living in other areas, have not been able to find successful roles in modern society. The process of change and modernization has brought a better life to only a few Bushmen.

It is clear that the old way of life as a hunting and gathering "bush" people is fast becoming a thing of the past. A number of Bushman children today attend school and are learning ways of adapting to a new economy. But their future as a cultural group is less sure.

There is still no clear policy regarding the Bushmen and the safeguarding of their future in the countries with large Bushman populations. Unless this situation changes soon, the Bushmen, as a people with a unique cultural identity, may be totally absorbed by other population groups.

Although elsewhere they have left behind a visible monument in the form of rock art, Bushmen may in time vanish from the Kalahari region without a trace. Hopefully, this will not happen. If it does, it will leave not only the Kalahari, but the whole of Africa, very much the poorer.

A woman from the northern Kalahari wrapped in her kaross.

Will the Bushmen continue to live in the Kalahari?

Glossary

Artifact A tool or work of art made by man.

Blesbok A type of antelope.

Borehole A hole drilled in the ground to search for water.

Bushveld A low level area in southern Africa, with scrub vegetation.

Commando Originally an Afrikaans word for a small armed force on horseback.

Drakensberg A mountain range in southern Africa.

Duiker A small type of antelope.

Eland A large, spiral-horned antelope believed to have had a special symbolic significance to prehistoric Bushmen.

Extended family A family that includes grandparents, uncles, aunts and cousins.

Francolin An African partridge.

Gemsbok and **hartebeest** Large types of antelope.

Highveld The high-altitude grassland of the Transvaal.

Karoo The arid plateaus of western South Africa.

Kaross A cloak made of animal skin.

Khoi The *Khoi* are neighbors of some Bushmen groups but are herdsmen and not hunters.

Kin Relatives by blood or marriage.

Korhaan A South African game bird.

Kudu An antelope with spiral horns.

Labyrinth A maze or network.

Migrating When people, animals or birds move to different habitats at certain times of year.

Mongongo nut A staple food for Bushmen, from the mongongo or mangetti tree

Pestle and mortar Pestle, an instrument for pounding food in a bowl called a mortar.

Plant foods Plants that have nutritional value.

Population pressure When an expanding population requires more territory.

Puberty The period at the beginning of adolescence.

San A name used by the *Khoi* to describe Bushmen.

Sandveld Desert.

Savanna Open grasslands.

Springbok An antelope that inhabits semi-desert regions of southern Africa.

Steenbok A small antelope of southern Africa.

Trance A dream-like state.

Tubers Plants with short, thick underground stems.

Warthog A wild pig with large tusks.

Wildebeest A sturdy type of antelope that migrates regularly in huge herds. Also called gnu.

Bushman languages

Bushman languages differ, but they all have click sounds. There are five of these sounds, which are written with the symbols !, /, //, ≠ and θ.

Clicks:

! The alveolar-palatal (or palatal) click, which is made by quickly bringing the tip of the tongue away from the palate above the upper front teeth.

/ The dental click. This is made by sucking the tip of the tongue back from the inside of the upper teeth.

// The lateral click — made by quickly bringing the sides of the tongue away from the roof of the mouth.

≠ The alveolar click. This is made by quickly bringing the upper surface of the tongue away from the roof of the mouth.

θ The bilabial click, found only in languages spoken in the southern Kalahari. This is made by pushing the lips together and then quickly pulling them apart.

Books to read

Kalahari Hunter-Gatherers: Studies of the Kung and Their Neighbors by Richard B. Lee and Irwin DeVare (Harvard University Press, 1976).

The Creative Patterns in Primitive Africa by Laurens van de Post (Spring Publications, 1987)

Testament to the Bushman by Laurens van der Post and Jane Taylor (Viking, 1985).

The Life and Words of a Kung Woman by Marjorie Shostak (Harvard University Press, 1981).

Harmless People by Elizabeth M. Thomas (Random, 1965).

Phontic and Phonological Studies of the Bushmen by Anthony Trail (Helmut Bushe Verlag Hamburg, 1985).

The Bushmen by Alfred Wannenburg (Smith Publications, 1982).

NISA: The Life and Words of a Kung Woman (Random, 1982).

Picture acknowledgments

All the photographs appearing in this book were supplied by the author, except on the following pages: 10, by Etienne du Pisani; 13, 14, 16 by Mansell Collection; 12, 15, 25, 42 by Wayland Picture Library. The map on page 6 is by Malcolm Walker. The cover picture is by H.P. Steyn.

© Copyright 1985 Wayland (Publishers) Ltd.
61 Western Road, Hove, East Sussex
BN3 1JD, England

Index